TOMORROW'S SCIENCE

Artificial Intelligence

Anne Rooney

Chrysalis Children's Books

Artificial Intelligence
Genetic Engineering
Internet Technologies
Medicine Now

Visit the Chrysalis website
www.chrysalisbooks.co.uk
for teachers' notes to
accompany this series.

First published in the UK in 2003 by
Chrysalis Children's Books,
64 Brewery Road London N7 9NT

Editor:	Susie Brooks
Designer:	John Jamieson
Consultant:	Helen Cameron
Picture researcher:	Jenny Barlow

Also thanks to: Gill Adams, Senior Inspector, CEA@Islington; Pip Hardy; Penny Worms

Anne Rooney asserts her moral right to be recognised as the author of this work.
If you have any comments on this book, please email her at anne@annerooney.co.uk.
For more information on her work, visit www.annerooney.co.uk.

ISBN 184138 868 8

British Library Cataloguing in Publication Data for this book is available from the British Library.

A BELITHA BOOK

Printed in Hong Kong

Picture acknowledgements
All reasonable efforts have been made to trace the relevant copyright holders of the images contained within this book. If we were unable to reach you, please contact Chrysalis Children's Books.

B = bottom; *L* = left; *R* = right; *T* = top

Cover (girl) Rex/Vic Thomasson (robot) Reuters/Kimimasa Mayama 1 The Kobal Collection/MGM 4 Mary Evans 5 Rex/Steve Lyne 6 Rex/MFT 7 *T* Corbis/Sygma/Martin Greg *B* The Kobal Collection/Lucasfilm/20th Century Fox 8 Rex/Chris Martin Bahr 9 SPL/Eurelios/Delphine Aures 10 The Kobal Collection/MGM 11 The Kobal Collection/ Lucasfilm/Hamshere, Keith 12 (see cover) 13 Hulton Archive 14 The Kobal Collection/MGM 15 (see 1) 16 The Kobal Collection/Paramount Television 17 Rex/Sipa 18 Rex/C. Laruffa 19 The Kobal Collection/Amblin Dreamworks/Stanley Kubrick/WB/James, David 20 SPL/Sam Ogden 21 *T* The Kobal Collection/Paramount Television *B* Corbis Saba/Tom Wagner 22 RSPCA Photolibrary/D. Dedeurwaerdere 23 The Kobal Collection/Walt Disney Pictures 24 Rex/Roy Garne 25 Rex/Timepix/Ted Thai 26 The Kobal Collection/Carolco 27 The Kobal Collection/ Dimension Films/Torres, Rico 28 Hulton 29 and 30 Corbis/Bettmann 31 Rex/Action Press 32 Mary Evans 33 The Kobal Collection/Touchstone/Bray, Phil 34 Corbis/Jon Feingersh 35 *T* (see cover) *B* SPL/CC Studio 36 Corbis 37 The Kobal Collection/Warner Bros 38 Corbis/Bohemian Picturemakers 39 *T* Corbis/Owen Franken *B* Rex/Sipa 40 *T* Rex/Allover Press *B* Corbis/Ethan Miller 41 Chrysalis Images 42 Reuters/Kimimasa Mayama 43 and 44 SPL/Peter Menzel 45 Paul Wright.

Contents

Introducing AI

Most people think of intelligence in terms of how clever a person is. But what do we really mean by intelligence? Can we measure it? Can we develop it or are we born with it? And can we create intelligence in something else, such as a machine?

Artificial intelligence

Artificial intelligence (AI) is all about creating machines that are 'clever' – that can think for themselves, communicate and act in some of the same ways as humans. Truly intelligent machines do not yet exist, but scientists are busy working to develop this new generation of computers and a lot of money is invested in the research.

In this book we'll look at movements in AI research, and think about some of the questions that this new technology raises. There are many difficult but intriguing issues about how far AI technology could and should go, and whether the benefits will outweigh the possible problems. We must all think about these things if we are to play an active part as citizens and have a say in how our world develops.

A very early idea of AI appears in Jewish legends of the Golem. A Golem was an automated servant, made from clay, which could be brought to life by placing a magic token in its mouth. Removing the token would return the Golem to clay.

This book won't tell you what to think. It will give you some technical background and suggest many different views and possibilities. Then you can think about and discuss the issues, forming your own opinions – opinions that you are able to explain and defend.

What is intelligence?

In order to make sense of AI, we need to understand what intelligence is, how it can be created in a machine and why we would want to do this. There is no agreed definition of intelligence, but most people accept that it involves being able to:

- learn from experiences
- understand and use information
- make sensible decisions, even in unfamiliar situations
- anticipate the consequences of events and actions.

There are other factors too, such as emotions, consciousness, awareness of other people, and a moral or ethical sense. So how can we create all this in a computer?

Exams usually test knowledge, skills and memory rather than intelligence. A computer could be programmed to do well in exams, but would that make it intelligent?

AI research

Leading the research into AI is the Massachussetts Institute of Technology (MIT). Scientists there are working on computers that can learn, see, talk and move around sensibly (by learning where obstacles are and avoiding them). The scientists are trying to find out what qualities a machine needs to do these things – but their work is not purely for research. They hope that by conquering AI they'll be able to build something useful with a wide range of functions. This will have many implications for us; we'll explore some of them in this book.

Definition: ethics

Ethics is the study of what is right and wrong. Some people believe there is an absolute code of ethics – things 'are' right or wrong – and others think that we make up our own ethical codes, which will be different in different societies. In this book we'll discuss the ethics of AI.

5

How could we use AI?

Because there are likely to be many uses for AI, scientists aim to develop different systems to suit different functions.

Soon we're likely to see very advanced software that can work with huge amounts of information and reach intelligent conclusions. This could be done on computers that look no different from those we use every day. We may well develop robots that look mechanical but can move independently and get information from their surroundings

A lawyer can use an expert system to access details about every court case ever recorded. The machine holds more information than the lawyer's memory can, but so far only a human has the imagination to use the knowledge effectively.

by seeing, touching and hearing in a similar way to humans. One day, we could have 'living' robots that look, talk, move and act just like we do.

Expert systems

A computer can 'know' more than a human can. It can deal with many facts at once, comparing details and making judgements more quickly and thoroughly than we can. There are already computer systems that use specialised knowledge to try to solve problems. The most advanced of these are called expert systems. A medical expert system might play the part of a doctor, able to compare quickly a patient's symptoms and medical history with a huge database of illnesses.

Features and function

Many AI robots will look nothing like living beings because this might put them at a disadvantage. Some AI robots will have wheels or other special tools that are more effective than human features at performing certain tasks. But some AI systems may be built to look like people or animals. We'd react very differently to an AI being that looked like a person rather than, say, a fridge.

Robot capabilities

You might think it would be great to have a robot to clean your shoes and make your tea. But would a robot ever give you unhealthy food like crisps, or accept that your trainers are more trendy when they're grubby?

The potential for AI is particularly great in rescue work, where environments may be too dangerous for humans to work in.

This would need a human touch, but so far computers can't take account of details that they haven't been 'taught' or told how to deal with.

To count as an AI being (often called just an AI) a machine must be able to learn and think. But, as we'll see later, some may eventually have consciousness, creativity, emotions, and a moral sense, too.

Androids, like C3PO from *Star Wars*, are robots with a human form. So far, androids still have a mechanical look which reminds us that they're not real people.

Introducing AI
Making intelligent machines

To create a machine that can think, act and interact in a way that's useful to us is a very complex task. In order to achieve this, scientists working on AI need to understand as much as possible about the human brain and behaviour. This is a huge challenge, as there is still a lot we don't know about how our own minds work.

Just like us?

We tend to take for granted many of our abilities. Most of us can:
- ◆ work with information from our senses to understand the world around us
- ◆ move around as we want, coordinating our bodies to do so
- ◆ communicate with other people using language
- ◆ use unrelated pieces of information to make sensible decisions.

We don't usually think of all these things as indicators of intelligence – they're just part of being human. Not all AIs will need to do every one of these things – but they'll all need to do some. And a machine will need to be constructed and programmed very carefully to give it these complicated skills.

Independent thought

Traditional computer programs use logic and clear instructions to find the answer to a question. This isn't how people think most of the time, and it isn't how we will make AI systems. An AI will need to be able to learn so that it can go beyond its original programming. The ability to learn is vital if a machine is to be capable of independent thought.

So far, the most intelligent machine is not even as smart as a slug!

Neural networks

Humans learn from experience and observation. We compare new situations with past ones, and this helps us to decide how to act. AIs will need to do the same.

Artificial neural networks are computer systems that copy the way the human brain works. They are good at working with language, shape recognition and tasks that need 'thinking'. Neural networks are at the heart of AI research.

Proving intelligence

You may have come across IQ tests that judge your ability to think quickly and to see connections between things. These aren't a great measure of intelligence – and they only apply to people. So how do we prove intelligence in a machine?

Several tests for intelligence in machines have been suggested. One of the most famous is the Turing test, named after the mathematician Alan Turing. He suggested that a machine could be called intelligent if a person communicating with it couldn't tell that it was a machine. There is an annual competition that challenges AIs in this way, and a prize is given for the best one.

As we've moved closer to creating AI systems, many scientists have decided that the Turing test isn't enough to prove a machine's intelligence – but it's a good start.

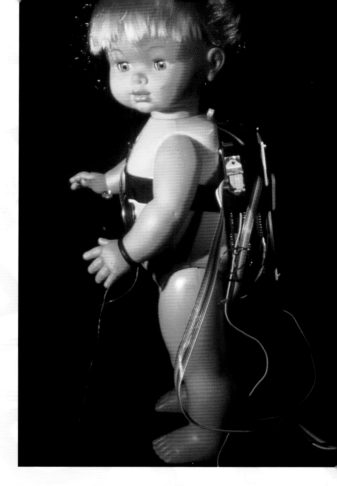

This robot doll is controlled by an artificial neural network that enables it to dance by linking tunes to movements. It can also learn simple sentences.

'Not until a machine can write a sonnet or compose a concerto because of thoughts and emotions felt… could we agree that machine equals brain – that is, not only write it, but know that it had written it.'

SIR GEOFFREY JEFFERSON,
PROFESSOR OF NEURAL SURGERY,
MANCHESTER UNIVERSITY, 1949

What's it to you?

Why should you worry about progress in AI? Isn't real AI too far in the future to matter? Not really – now's the time to think about it. Progress in all areas of science affects each of us in some way. Here are a few questions to think about as you read the rest of this book.

What are the risks?

Many areas of research may hold dangers we know nothing of at the moment. If we make something more intelligent than ourselves, it isn't clear that we will be able to control it. We may find that the intelligence of our machines grows more quickly than we had intended. What then?

Are there other issues?

Imagine a world in which there are intelligent machines among us. Will it alter our view of what it is to be human? How we see ourselves and judge our own intelligence might change if a machine could think, feel, have opinions and become better at some things than we are. Maybe our idea of the meaning, nature and value of life will change if we can make life, or something very like life, ourselves.

In the film *Westworld* (1973), AI androids built for entertainment turn against people. Is it right – or safe – to try to make something we don't fully understand?

Who's in charge?

Technological developments are largely in the hands of the developed world. People working on AI are likely to build systems that reflect the ideas, values and interests of their own countries – but how AI is developed and used may affect the whole world.

People in countries that aren't technologically advanced won't have any say in how AI is used – and even in the countries that are developing AI, many people will be left in the dark. The technology is very complicated, and the questions it raises are difficult. Who will make sure people are given the information they need to make choices and to voice their opinions?

What's 'good'?

We may agree to use AI only for good, but people have different ideas of what is 'good'. Suppose that, after the destruction of the World Trade Center in 2001, the USA had been able to use

Could AI warfare become a reality as in the film *Star Wars Episode I: Phantom Menace* (1999)?

AIs to destroy terrorist leader Osama bin Laden. Would they have done it? Should they have? Your answer will depend on who and where you are.

Over to you

We all have a right to be involved in decisions about the world's future. But to have the power to change things, we need to understand the issues that affect us all. You will need to be able to separate fact from opinion in the things you read and hear. You will need to be able to disentangle reliable information from media scare stories and public relations hype. If you can do this, and shape your own informed views, you will be able to play an important part in the changing world. Use the 'Ask yourself' boxes in the following chapters as a starting point for discussing the issues raised.

Living machines?

It's pretty obvious, at the moment, that machines aren't alive. But sometimes we still talk about them as though they were. How often have you heard someone say 'My car's dead'? Whether we can make a truly living machine depends on how we define life. If our machines could think for themselves and work independently without us, could we still say they're not living? We might decide that an AI is 'alive' in some sense. What rights would a thinking, living machine have?

What counts as alive?

Think about what it means to be alive, and then decide whether any alternative forms of life are possible – either as things we could make or perhaps as beings from another part of the universe. It's a hard task.

A virus is a very simple organism. Scientists argue about whether it counts as something that's alive. However, like humans, it has a genome – genetic coding that acts as a 'recipe' for it. We can now make a virus by building it from chemicals strung together in the right order. An artificial virus behaves in exactly the same way as a naturally occurring

Alive and kicking – or just kicking? This Sony robot is still a machine. But as AI develops, we need to decide what qualities would make a robot 'living'.

one. If we count a virus as a living system, we can – just – make artificial life already.

Playing God

Some people may have religious objections to making something that's intelligent – especially if we can't agree whether it's alive. Many people with religious beliefs say that creating life is something only God can do. They may also say that it's blasphemous to 'play God' – to act like God ourselves and presume that we can create life. Some people believe that we don't die when our physical bodies cease to work, but our consciousness passes on to a new life – maybe as a person or maybe as another life form. This consciousness might be called a spirit, or a soul, or given another name. Do you think an AI can or will have a spirit?

Ask yourself

◆ Will an AI be a living being?
◆ Do you think it is wrong to try to create a living being?
◆ What should we do with a created living being that is no longer useful, or has broken?

Many religions have creation stories that explain how living beings came to exist in the first place. Should AIs be told how they came to exist?

In the novel *Frankenstein* by Mary Shelley, a scientist makes a creature out of parts of dead bodies. He makes it walk, talk and act like a living person. The novel raises issues of whether the creature is really alive, of its sense of self and what it means to be a person.

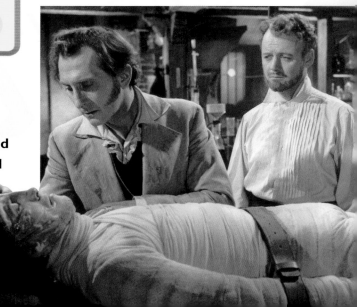

Living machines?

Know your rights

Every living person has rights, and in many countries some animals have rights, too. As a person, some of your rights – to food and shelter for example – are recognised worldwide and confirmed in the United Nations Universal Declaration of Human Rights. In most countries, national laws set out the rights people have to education, to vote in elections, to choose who to marry and so on.

If we build an AI being, will it have rights, too? This is a very far-reaching question, and we may decide that different types of AIs have different rights. Something that can think, that is aware of its own existence and that can feel pain or sorrow should perhaps have rights. Something that can work out how to make a better bridge but has no feelings maybe shouldn't have rights. We need to consider what rights any created intelligence will have and what duties we may have towards it before we create our AI beings.

Death of a machine?

If we decide that an intelligent machine is a life form, we have problems if we want to turn it off. We may feel it has the right to continue existing – or it may even decide that for itself. To turn it off might be seen as murder.

The Tin Man in *The Wizard of Oz* goes to the wizard because he wants a heart. Will our thinking machines have emotions?

Dave the astronaut takes apart HAL the computer in *2001: A Space Odyssey*. HAL seems afraid. Could a computer ever feel real fear as humans feel it?

Conscious machines

Consciousness is the ability to be aware of yourself. We don't know what makes us conscious, or where (if anywhere) in our bodies our consciousness is. We don't know if other creatures have consciousness, though it seems quite likely that other intelligent animals may have some form of it. Some creatures that work together – like ants and bees – may have a kind of group consciousness.

As we haven't yet made a machine that is conscious or can think, we don't know how it will behave when we do. We might find it develops consciousness automatically. If this is the case, we will need to decide whether we have any right to limit its ability to think and be aware of itself.

'I think, therefore I am.'

RENÉ DESCARTES, 1637

Ask yourself

◆ What rights do you think an AI should have, if any?
◆ Does it have a right to learn?
◆ Does it have the right to own things or have a say in what it does?
◆ If it feels emotion, should we be as kind and thoughtful towards it as we would be towards a human?

(15)

Facing feelings

Our feelings and our ability to imagine how other people think and feel help us to work together and get along with other people. If we created living beings without feelings, would we run into trouble?

How feelings are useful

During the course of each day, you feel many different emotions. You may be keen to get up or resentful at being woken. You may be excited about, or fearful of, something that you expect to happen. You might feel disappointed or joyful, angry, ashamed, amused, pleased...

In *Star Trek*, **Mr Spock is not an AI but a living being who feels no emotions. His great intelligence and grasp of logic, combined with his lack of feeling, make him like a living computer. There are many scenes in the series in which he is used to illustrate the limitations of logic alone.**

Your feelings affect how you behave. If you forget to feed your pet mouse and it dies, you feel sad and guilty. If you get another pet mouse you will be more likely to remember to feed it because of these feelings. If you do well at something or are kind to someone, you feel good about yourself. This motivates you to do well or act well again in the future.

Feelings are important in helping us to function in society, relate to other people and learn patterns of behaviour that are acceptable. If feelings are useful in helping us to learn, they would probably also be useful to a learning machine.

An AI machine developed to recover survivors from an earthquake might try harder to succeed if it felt bad when it didn't find survivors – or proud when it did.

Case study

People suffering from autism have difficulty relating to others. They find it hard to understand how other people may think or feel. Sometimes they can't form functional relationships with other people or make sense of the world around them. In extreme cases, they are completely shut off in a world of their own. It's possible that an AI might behave like this if it had no emotions – and it may act in a way that people have trouble relating to.

Ask yourself

◆ If we are able to build an intelligent machine with emotions, should we?
◆ Should we allow the machine to be pleased with itself if it does well?
◆ What about making it feel sorrow or guilt or pain if it makes a mistake or fails in the function it's intended for, such as rescuing people in an accident?
◆ Is it constructive to let a machine feel pain?

Facing feelings

Understanding feelings

The computer systems we have today work in a logical way – they use reason to find answers to problems. But the 'reasonable' answer to a problem is not always a workable or acceptable one. Even with an informed understanding of what is unacceptable, an intelligent machine will have difficulty with some of our more inconsistent behaviour. How would it act in 'one-off' situations?

An AI working by logic might decide to solve world hunger by killing 'surplus' people in areas that can't produce much food. Humans, with feelings, would consider this to be wrong. Would feeling compassion help AIs to act more acceptably?

Consider the following scenario. A person is very sick and in pain and he will certainly die in a short while. He asks his AI care assistant to kill him. Should the AI do it? Perhaps it would be kind, but it would also be illegal. Would this matter to an AI?

Creating feelings

One of our aims in building AIs should be that they don't harm people. To teach a machine what would harm people – physically or emotionally – would be difficult. The machine would also need the ability to anticipate how a person might react to something. It may be easier to give the machine feelings itself, letting it have a proper insight into how people think and feel.

Dangerous feelings

A machine without feelings or an understanding of human nature could make mistakes. It could be dangerous. But a machine with feelings might fall in love, have tantrums, panic, become bored, argue about what it was supposed to do or just sulk and do nothing! Machines go wrong, too. Imagine a computer virus that made all AIs depressed – or evil. A machine with emotions could be dangerous.

If we allowed our machines to have feelings, our duties towards them would be rather different, as well. We'd have to be polite and considerate and avoid upsetting or offending them. It would be bad not only for the AI but also for us as people if we treated a feeling machine badly.

Ask yourself

◆ If you hurt or upset an AI, what should it be able to do about it?
◆ Should it protect itself, even if that meant harming or upsetting a person?
◆ Or should we be able to treat an AI as we like, with no fear of the outcome?

In the film *AI* (2001) David is an experimental AI boy who is programmed to love his mother absolutely and for ever. She abandons him, and he spends 2000 years searching for her, never able to sleep, die or give up. Should it be possible to condemn an AI to such a terrible fate?

Bio-bots and cyborgs

It's fairly easy to think of robots as machines, as long as they remain obviously mechanical. But if we make robots that have a skin-like covering, or fur or other animal attributes, we may find it harder to recognise them as machines. Work is underway not only to build bio-bots – robots with soft tissues like human flesh – but also to create cyborgs by giving real people and animals robotic functions.

Bodies and brains

We all know that it's not just our bodies that make us human – our minds are really what make us ourselves. So we probably won't demand that an AI looks like us before we accept its intelligence and character. Indeed, researchers have found that people are keen to interact and form bonds with even very artificial-looking robots.

However, giving a robot some similarity to the human form, such as two 'eyes' and an upright stance, helps us to relate to it.

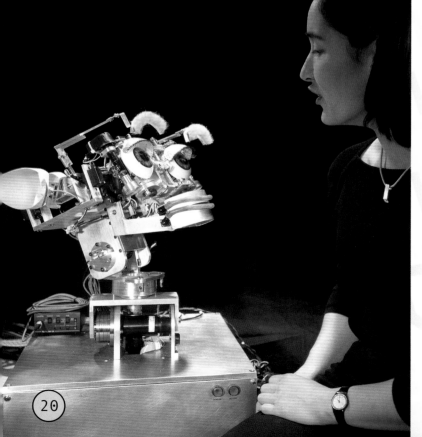

Researchers have found that however unlike a human being a robot looks, we will warm to it if it engages our interest in some way – for example, if it responds to us with different expressions.

Some science fiction androids look very like humans. In *Star Trek: The Next Generation*, Data is singled out only by his strangely coloured eyes.

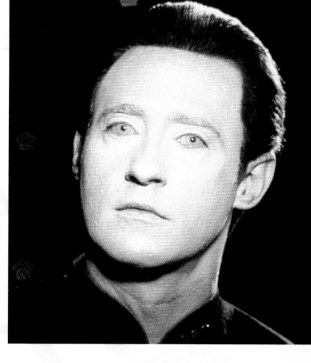

Soft-bodied robots

We would probably respond best to a robot that seemed to have skin and hair and to move its body in the same ways that we move. Scientists are working on machines that might be powered by the sugar glucose, like our own bodies, and that have a soft tissue covering like skin. They could have artificial muscles and be capable of quite realistic movement.

A research group at MIT is working on using real muscle, from genetically modified animals, in robots. They are experimenting with using whole muscles and cultured muscle grown from cells outside the body of the original animal. If a robot, bio-bot or android looked identical to a human, we might find it difficult to remember that it's

not really a person. We might form relationships with it, pin our expectations and hopes on it and be disappointed if it didn't return our interest or affection.

Japan has an ageing population and low birthrate – soon there won't be enough nursing staff to look after the elderly. AI androids could act as care nurses. But would we trust them as much as we would a person?

Ask yourself

◆ Making 'robots' with living tissue and giving them intelligence is close to making life itself. Is it a boundary that shouldn't be crossed, or could developing intelligent humanoid robots solve many problems in today's society?

Machine or animal?

Cybernetics is a branch of technology that explores control mechanisms in artificial and biological systems. Scientists in this field are starting to add electronic components to some animals. This is not, at the moment, moving towards creating AI animals, but is going the other way – taking a real animal and adapting it with technology to suit our needs.

In Tokyo, researchers have found a way to fit a cockroach with an electronic device that can be remotely controlled and used to move the insect's legs. The electrical impulse in the legs is the same as it would be if it came from the cockroach's own nervous system, and it causes the cockroach to walk in the direction the controller wants it to go in. This technology has also been tested on rats.

Ask yourself

◆ Is it right to take over the body of a living thing – even if it's as humble as a cockroach – and treat it like a machine?
◆ Is it fair to use some animals in this way but not others? If so, how would you decide which animals could be used?
◆ Would it matter what the technology was used for?
◆ Would you consider giving your own pet an electronic implant, perhaps to track it if it was lost or stolen?

A remotely controlled rat could be used to carry a bomb to a target or transport a mini camera into rubble after a disaster. If your family were buried in earthquake wreckage, would you think it acceptable to send a rat to find them?

Kevin Warwick, Professor of Cybernetics at the University of Reading, is a cyborg – part human, part machine. He has had small electronic devices fitted into his body and connected to his nervous system. The first implant meant that he could be tracked around a building and doors would open and lights turn on as he approached. The second linked his nervous system to the Internet, and the third enabled him to control a robot arm on the other side of the Atlantic. He hopes eventually to be able to download his feelings and thoughts and store them in a computer. He also aims to communicate directly with other people with similar devices – his wife now has an implant, too, to help him experiment.

In the movie *Inspector Gadget* (1999) a man horribly injured in an accident is rebuilt with lots of mechanical components, giving him powers no normal person could develop. A villain steals the technology and makes a violent and destructive copy of him.

Superhuman powers

If cybernetics were taken to extremes, there's a chance that people could gain 'superhuman' abilities by having electronic implants. They may be able to communicate using telepathy and alleviate pain without drugs. This idea could be used in many areas, from reading the minds of criminal suspects to communicating with deaf, blind or paralysed people.

Ask yourself

◆ How should we deal with the possibility of this kind of technology being abused – for listening in to people's thoughts, perhaps, or making super-powerful soldiers or inflicting pain?
◆ Should we restrict research or impose safeguards?

Designs on the future

Computers are very good at tasks that require logic and calculations – they are already better than people at this type of work. This means they can play a valuable role in helping to design other computers. An intelligent computer would be even better at helping us to design and build improved AI computers. But could it be that we're only safe as long as the designing and building of AIs stays in human hands?

Man versus machine

MIT is already working on systems that will get help from computers on designs for intelligent machines. They hope to build design systems that will allow engineers to 'chat' with a computer using a whiteboard,

Already, one type of machine can be used to build another. Robots like this could soon be building more robots as well as cars.

MIT professor Rodney Brooks has developed an AI robot called 'Cog' that attempts to program and reprogram itself by interacting with people and objects. If it perfects this, it may one day be able to program other AIs.

drawing sketches and sharing ideas that would normally be discussed with other people. The computer would ask intelligent questions, make calculations and suggestions and may soon be able to say how a better computer could be built.

At the moment, we think about the purpose of a new machine and design it accordingly. But computers may come up with very different designs or purposes. Their own 'idea' for an improved model or machine may not always match ours.

Who's responsible?

If someone is harmed by a badly designed item, the designer or manufacturer is liable. This means that they are held responsible and may have to pay compensation to the person who's been hurt.

If an expert system were to design something faulty, we could hold the manfacturer of the item responsible or the designer of the expert system. But once we have intelligent systems designing things, and even designing further intelligent systems, it becomes

more complicated. Any limitations in the design or programming of the first system may lead to more and more errors in future 'generations' of AI systems.

Ask yourself

◆ Imagine an AI scarecrow that has been designed by an AI farming system to kill crows. What happens if it kills a rare bird of a protected species? Who's responsible? The farmer? The AI scarecrow? The AI farming system? The designer of the AI farming system?

Designs on the future

Robot rule

A world in which computers or robots have taken over from humans is common in science fiction books and films. Some people fear we are building a world where this is possible.

If we create an AI system that can design other AIs, and improve on its own powers, it's possible that it will begin to think about the role of people in the world. War, famine, cruelty and destruction of the environment are evils that an intelligent system would want to end. Following logic alone, AI systems could well decide that we've done a poor job of managing the planet and that they could do better. They might even be right.

The film *Terminator* (1984) shows a future world that's run by destructive robots. Movies like this play on our fears that robots or AIs could take over the world and destroy us.

Are we safe?

It might seem foolish to think that intelligent machines could ever take over from us. Is it just a nightmare scenario, or could it be a real threat?

Researchers into AI are divided over this question. Some argue that we are safe because we control the power and manufacture of the machines – we can cut their power supply or stop building them, for example. Others say that as AIs will be able to communicate, using the Internet or an equivalent, they will be able to control the power networks and will be smart enough to avoid our attempts at stopping them. We are so dependent on computer-controlled systems that we

In *Spy Kids* (2001) an evil genius creates androids with which he intends to take over the world. His plan fails when two children reverse the programming so that the androids turn good. AIs will have the potential to be good or evil, depending on how they're used.

could well be held to ransom by machines that could, for example, detonate bombs, immobilise the police or cause economic disaster.

Crime and terror

Even if we keep strict control over what AIs are able to design and build, criminals and terrorists are always quick to use technology for their own ends. If we make it possible to create AIs that can design and build new AIs to a set of requirements or a 'recipe', we can't be sure that it won't be turned against us. A terrorist, a military leader – or even a teenage hacker or virus writer – might be able to create AIs that could cause havoc. For AIs to be useful to us, they must be powerful – but this could make them dangerous in the wrong hands.

Ask yourself

◆ Once AI machines are able to design other machines, are they likely to design things that will help robots rule?
◆ How could we guard against this?

Case study

Computers that are used to buy and sell shares on the world's stock markets were partly to blame for the economic crash called 'Black Monday' in 1987. The systems were allowed to make their own decisions. Because they work much faster than people, they quickly sold shares, pushing the prices down. As the prices fell, more computers sold shares, making the prices fall even further. If people had been making the decisions, the fall would have been slower and they'd have spotted what was happening.

Ethical machines

Intelligent systems that make decisions for us can't work without guidance about what we consider right and wrong. Whenever we make a decision, we take into account lots of different factors. Many of these are ethical or moral issues, so intelligent systems will need to have a good grasp of these, too.

About ethics

Ethics is all about right and wrong. In some cases, many people agree, and some ethical issues are built into laws. So most people agree that we shouldn't kill each other, or take each other's property. Murder and theft are illegal in every country. But there's disagreement over some ethical issues. Most vegetarians believe it is wrong to eat animals, for instance, but other people don't have a problem with this. In some cases, there are cultural, religious or regional differences. In the West, most people believe we should be allowed to marry who we wish, but in some other countries arranged

During World War I, people went to prison for refusing to join the war and kill people. Their belief that killing is wrong was seen as going against the national interest and considered cowardly and selfish.

CONSCIENTIOUS OBJECTORS

marriages between strangers are common and acceptable.

Occasionally, we may make exceptions to our beliefs in particular circumstances. Some people (even if they agree that it's wrong to kill) feel it's acceptable to help someone to die if they're in terrible pain and have asked to die. Some people believe a death penalty – killing someone guilty of a serious crime – is acceptable, and some countries still have a death penalty.

Developing ethical codes

Over time, societies develop systems of what they think is right and wrong. Ethical codes aren't thought up by someone at one stroke – they evolve. Our ideas of right and wrong generally help society to run smoothly. Where there is disagreement, there may be debate or conflict. In some cases, there can be war or revolution.

The 18th-century philosopher Immanuel Kant believed there is a universal moral law that is the same for all people.

Ask yourself

◆ Do you think some things are always right or wrong? Or does it depend on the society or country you live in?
◆ Can what's right and wrong change over time?

Ethics for machines

We clearly need an ethical code for an intelligent system that can make decisions. Otherwise, it will follow its own logic and may come up with unacceptable solutions. A human

politician would be unlikely to consider saving money on healthcare by letting seriously ill people die without offering treatment. But a machine trying to make decisions based on logic might find this the most efficient answer.

As we don't all agree on what's right and wrong, it will be difficult to agree on the ethical code we give to intelligent machines.

Ask yourself

◆ Who can we trust to put together an ethical code that will be used by AIs?
◆ Will all AIs use the same code?

Ethics by machines

Machines that are more intelligent than us – or have more 'thinking power' than us – will probably be able to analyse and refine the ethical code we give them. As they're bound to be able to communicate with each other, they'll also be able to share 'ideas' on ethics.

There might be some things that an AI will refuse to do if it thinks about right and wrong. An AI will apply its ethical code rigorously, whereas people are swayed by self-interest, feeling sympathy or pity and even by moods such as laziness. The AI's rigour may often be an advantage. But an AI may not be able to show mercy or judge how a particular action will affect individual people.

Julius Robert Oppenheimer was one of the scientists who made the atomic bomb possible. Could an AI foresee the outcome of such research and refuse to participate?

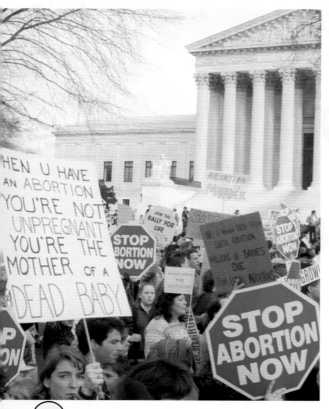

Some issues provoke heated debate as people try to persuade others of their views. How might we feel about arguing with an AI? Should it be programmed so that it can't change its views?

Ethics and religions

Some ethical codes are closely tied to religious beliefs. In many countries, people are allowed to follow any religion they wish, and the law tries to support them in practising their faith. In other places, there is one religion that is approved by the state and other religions are banned. Presumably, these countries would want their AI systems to live by their religious and ethical codes.

It's possible that an intelligent system, with information about different religions and beliefs, may be able to say that one or another is 'right' or 'true'. This would have very serious consequences for us all. Perhaps an AI system may adopt a religion and reject its original programming. Or it may even start its own religion.

Many humans rely on religious faith. Might an AI want to practise a religion?

31

Ethical machines

Bias in AI systems

It is very difficult for people to make unbiased decisions – decisions not influenced by their own feelings, opinions or interests.

In some areas, we may think we aren't biased as everyone we know would make the same choice. But we may be showing a national or cultural bias. Everyone you know would probably agree that boys and girls have equal rights to education. But this is not held to be true everywhere. A view such as this, built into an AI system, would be accepted in the West but deemed to be biased, or an error, if it was applied in some other countries.

Ask yourself

◆ Is it possible to create an AI that has no bias if we are biased ourselves?
◆ If we did succeed, might a thinking machine develop its own bias anyway?
◆ As most AIs will probably be built in the West, will nations with different views want to buy them?
◆ Should the West willingly create AIs with different value systems?

The Buddhist view that we should live our lives causing as little harm as possible might be a good principle for AIs to follow. But would human nature allow us to program an AI so selflessly?

Conscience and free will

An AI equipped with a thorough ethical code would be programmed to follow it – it wouldn't have a choice. It wouldn't need a conscience to guide it morally unless it could choose its actions freely – it had free will. It would be dangerous to give AIs free will and the ability to ignore their programming, but it might happen if someone tried it as an experiment, if a virus or hacker 'broke' an AI system, or if AIs found flaws that let them reject their programming. Free will without a conscience is dangerous – think, for example, of murderers who kill without thinking it's wrong.

In *Bicentennial Man* (1999), a robot spends 200 years trying to become a human with his own free will.

Case study

In the fairy story and Disney movie *Pinocchio*, a wooden boy puppet is magically brought to life. Although he can walk and talk, he isn't a real boy and goes on a quest to become one. He's given an external - artificial - conscience to help him decide what's good and bad. At the very end of the tale, a fairy turns him into a real boy because he's chosen to be good. He's been given free will, used it well and followed his conscience, and this has made him 'alive'.

Ask yourself

- ◆ Would AIs want to be 'real' people?
- ◆ Would they know if they were?
- ◆ Would we know?

Do you know who you're talking to?

When you use a telephone, you often end up talking to a machine. You might leave a message on an answerphone or someone's voice mail, or you may use the keys on your phone to book tickets or find out information using a computer system. Once we develop intelligent systems, there may be many more situations in which people interact with machines.

If you couldn't tell if the voice at a call centre was a machine or a person, would it matter?

Robo-teacher

One area in which AI is likely to be used relatively early on in its development is education. Imagine a teacher who knows everything, has superb teaching skills, has many approaches to learning that it can adapt to suit your needs – and that never gets tired of explaining the same point again and again. It could be perfect. But would an AI have the same enthusiasm as your teacher? Would it care how well you progress? Would it have a sense of humour or be able to surprise you?

For some learning activities, computers are very successful. Could they take over the role of classroom teachers?

Robo-medics

AIs could also manage many of the day-to-day tasks handled by medical staff. How would patients feel about this? A person who needs constant care may have a close bond with their human carer. On the other hand, they may feel guilty and resentful. An AI may be better for some people – but we'd need to assess each person's needs carefully. This can be a difficult and costly process; if we got it wrong, vulnerable people might suffer by losing the human contact they need.

A medical expert system can't yet perform all the functions of a human doctor, who uses instinct and observation as much as the patient's description of his or her symptoms. Could a machine ever replace this?

Ask yourself

◆ How would you feel about being taught by a computer or robot?
◆ Would it matter to you whether it looked and acted like a person?
◆ Do you think person-to-person jobs – being a mentor, a companion or an advisor – could be taken on by an AI?

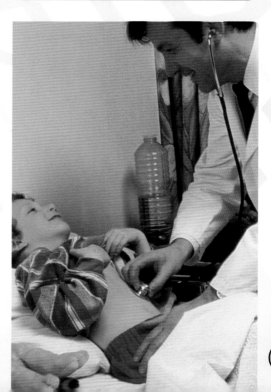

Do you know who you're talking to?

Talking things over

Many people find that talking to a trained counsellor or psychotherapist helps them with their problems. This might be a task you think a machine couldn't possibly do. But you may be wrong. Recent trials of computerised therapy systems have often had very positive results. People seem to feel that they can keep their dignity intact and preserve their privacy if they talk to a machine instead of a person.

Maybe telephone or online help-desks could use AI systems to deal with calls – they often have too many calls for their human operators to deal with anyway. Would this work?

Case study

In 1966, a computer system called Eliza was programmed to act like a therapist. It wasn't an AI – it used a simple questioning technique. Eliza responded to people's comments and questions with more questions, much as a human counsellor might do to get to the bottom of a person's problems. Eliza didn't understand the clients' feedback in any meaningful sense but used keywords to trigger questions that were usually suitable. To the surprise of researchers, Eliza was immensely popular.

Psychologists such as Sigmund Freud have helped people to think through their problems. Could AIs be programmed to do this?

AIs and privacy

We'd need to decide what should happen to the information given to a therapy AI, and what should or could be done with any conclusions the AI drew from it. There are strict rules about what a human doctor, therapist or priest can do with information given in confidence. We'd need similar, and additional, protection for people confiding in an AI which would also run the risk of being hacked into.

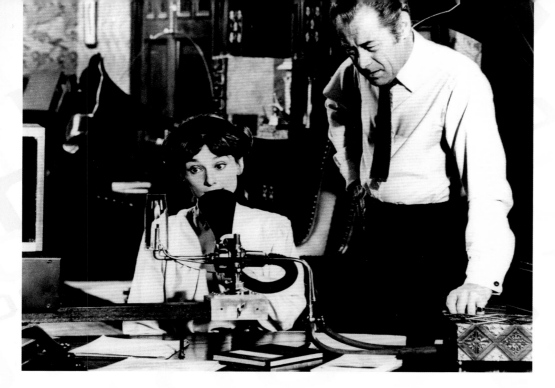

The therapy system Eliza was named after the character Eliza Dolittle in George Bernard Shaw's play *Pygmalion*. Working girl Eliza is 'programmed' to become a society lady by a professor of phonetics.

Ask yourself

◆ Would you trust the security of a computer system enough to share your innermost secrets with it?
◆ Should people have the right to know what conclusions an AI system has drawn about them and perhaps to challenge them?

Dealing with the unreal

Some people have difficulty accepting that the characters in the soap operas they see on television are not real people. They may write to or accost the actors, expecting them to be the characters they play. There could be similar difficulties for some people in recognising that a voice they talk to on the phone doesn't belong to a real person but is in fact a computer or AI system. If we ever get to the stage of having androids, the issue will become very difficult as it may not always be possible to tell if the 'person' facing you is human at all.

Ask yourself

◆ Would you want to reveal intimate details about yourself to an AI being – either for medical reasons or to get help with an emotional problem?
◆ Should we have the right to know if we're talking to an AI or to choose to talk to a person instead?

AIs at work

When we build AIs, we will build them to serve us – to do jobs we don't want to do or can't do as well, as quickly or as cheaply. How will this change society?

Robot slaves?

There are many unpleasant and menial jobs that have to be done. These jobs usually fall to people with limited skills or a lack of choice. Often, immigrant workers and people who've achieved little success in formal education end up doing the jobs that no one else wants to do.

Many repetitive jobs in factories have already been taken over by machinery. These machines don't require any intelligence, but it could soon be possible for machines to take on different tasks. These may be the jobs that, although boring, dirty or unpleasant for a person to do, still need a set of skills that we can't yet give to a machine. They could include cleaning, fruit picking and some basic nursing tasks such as emptying bed pans. An intelligent machine may be much more efficient than a person, not needing holidays, breaks or time off due to illness.

Many factory workers were replaced by automated systems in the 20th century. What will happen as the 21st century progresses?

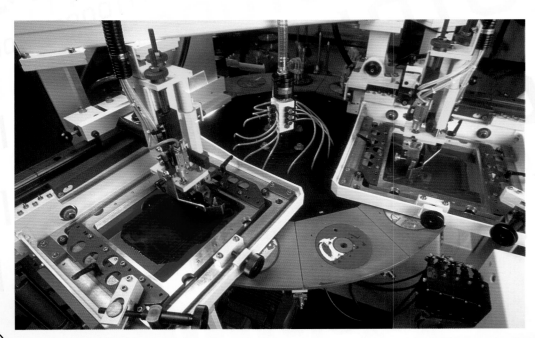

Might some workers lose the jobs they enjoy to AIs? How could we protect them?

Skilled workers

It's not only unskilled workers who may be replaced by AI systems. As expert systems in areas such as the law and medicine improve, they might take over some parts of the jobs of human experts. A doctor or lawyer may no longer need such detailed knowledge if they could call on an expert system to support their judgements or diagnoses.

Journalism is a skilled profession. Could we one day see AI news crews reporting on world events?

Case study

Columbia University in the USA is experimenting with an AI system to read and interpret news from several sources. The Columbia Newsblaster uses natural language processing to 'understand' the news and write its own report. It can't – yet – make links with other stories, place a story in a broader context or make other judgements that we expect from human journalists.

AIs at work

AI and creativity

It's already possible to get hold of very basic story-writing programs – you can try some out on the World Wide Web. And computers can put together simple bits of music. An AI system that could try out its compositions on people to see which they like, and analyse popular music or literature written by people, might come up with acceptable new entertainment. It would follow the rules, meet expectations and many people may enjoy the product. But it's unlikely that an AI system would come up with anything very original or striking, because it would be working from what it knows people like already.

Some modern pop bands have achieved success by copying aspects of music that people have liked in the past. Could these musicians one day be replaced by AIs that function in a similar way?

We think of skilled musicians as among the most gifted of people. But now that computers can play musical instruments perfectly, will we think less of this skill?

Ask yourself

◆ Would you want to watch a TV programme or read a book that had been entirely put together by an AI system?
◆ Would you view it differently from one produced by people, even if you knew they were following a certain formula?

AI warfare

One of the most dangerous jobs a person can do is serve as a soldier. What if we could avoid risking human lives in the military? The possible uses of AIs as soldiers are likely to be a driving force in getting funding for some areas of research and development. Science fiction movies have made us familiar with the idea of robot armies battling with each other. And already, the USA has experimented with war planes and other vehicles that don't need human pilots or drivers.

Millions died in the trenches during World War I. Could AI warriors prevent such an atrocity in the future? If a country could build robot soldiers that were able to take intelligent, independent military action, should it do so?

Ask yourself

◆ Would there be more or less chance of war and more or fewer human casualties if wars were fought by AIs?
◆ Would it mean that the most technologically advanced country would always win the war?
◆ What would happen to the AI killing machines once the war was over?

What about us?

Building AI systems in any great number would mean we'd have to change the way we think of our own intelligence and skills and our identity as people. AIs could produce new challenges to our emotional well-being, our sense of ourselves and our control over our own lives.

People are encouraged to love animals. Is forming a bond with an artificial pet good emotional training or potentially damaging?

Feeling for AIs

Robotic pets have been around for a while. They're electronic 'animals' with simple programming and some sensors and controls so that they seem to respond when you talk to or play with them. They're not AIs – but future models might be.

We won't stop at pets. We may see AI companions for people who need constant care. We might eventually be able to have AI versions of people we love who've left us – or who have died. In the film *AI* (2001), the robot child is modelled on the dead son of the director of the robotics company. And just as some people use an answerphone message recorded by a celebrity, we might have celebrity AIs in our control. Would you like to have Britney Spears tidy your room or Brad Pitt pump up your bike tyres?

If AIs couldn't be mean to us, leave us or hate us, we wouldn't need to treat them as well as we treat people, even if we were supposed to.

Ask yourself

◆ Would it be harmful for people to form emotional relationships with AIs?
◆ Would the freedom to be inconsiderate – even cruel – to AIs be bad for us?

Who's in control?

We will give AIs power to make some decisions for us. This already happens – we let computers decide whether someone is a good risk for a bank loan, for instance. As more and more decisions are taken by computers, our own involvement in running the world will decrease. Maybe we'll hand over too much responsibility to AIs once we trust their abilities. We could end up stranded if the AIs are immobilised by a virus or make a seriously bad decision. Too much reliance on a system we don't directly control can be dangerous.

Bad vibes

In all areas of technology, new advances have first been used for military purposes and entertainment. AI won't be any different. It's likely

Some people believe that violent video games encourage real violence. Will it be safe to play violent AI or virtual-reality games?

that AI systems – whether robots, androids or computer software – will be used for games with a violent or sexual content. As they can be very realistic, they will give some people the impression that they are doing these things 'for real' – and in a setting in which it is allowed.

Ask yourself

◆ Should we restrict the use of AI for games with a violent content?
◆ Is it wrong to allow people to take pleasure in cruelty, even if it's not real? Or could it be a harmless way for people to release their aggression?

Who cares?

Researchers into AI can do what they like. There are a few journals and discussion groups thinking about the ethical issues of AI, but there are no restrictions – or even plans for restrictions – imposed by law. Legislation (law-making) can't always keep up with the fast pace of scientific advances. Will problems arising from AI take us by surprise?

Ethics committees

Ethics committees are groups of people who meet to discuss the work carried out by scientists in research institutions and hospitals. Some of the members are subject experts, and some are philosophers with an interest in ethics or morals. At present, AI research and development doesn't need to refer to an ethics committee. Do you think it should?

A role for philosophers

A philosopher is someone who thinks about issues such as what is right and wrong, about how we define a person or intelligence and whether anything other than humans can be conscious. This type of work is very important to AI development and how we will view any AIs we have.

Philosophers are perhaps the best people to put together an ethical code for AIs – but they won't all agree on what it should be. And it's unlikely that they will be left to get on with the job, without input from people with political or economic interests.

The law

At the moment, it's too early for laws regarding AI to exist – but we will need them. Each country may draw up its own laws, and they're likely to be quite different. Just as there are now arguments about how far the Internet can be controlled globally, countries may disagree about what AIs can do. The problem is, since AIs will probably be able to communicate with one another internationally, regional laws may not be much use.

MIT is a leading force in AI development. As well as research labs like this, it has a division looking into the ethics of AI.

Breaking the law

We have to accept that once AI development is properly understood, not all AI use will be legal – there will always be people who break the law. They may use AIs in crime; they may abuse AIs; a terrorist group may make AI soldiers or guerillas.

We could even see a brand of 'logic terrorism' in which terrorists or countries at war use sophisticated arguments and logic to affect how an enemy's AI systems act. An AI that can learn and work things out for

Daniel Dennett is a philosopher who has done a lot of work on issues relating to AI. His opinion could be important in the future.

itself might be persuaded to reveal a country's defence strategy or make changes to how it acts. An AI programmed to put the safety of humanity at the top of its list of goals could easily take actions that would go against an individual country's security interests.

Ask yourself

◆ Is AI so risky that we shouldn't proceed with the research?
◆ If we do go ahead, how much trust should we put in AIs?
◆ How far should we limit the things AIs can do without referring to humans?

Your own opinion

By now you should have enough background knowledge to start to form your own views on AI. These may be the same as, or different from, your friends'. But keep asking questions and finding things out. Try to understand all sides of the story. The more you learn, the stronger your arguments will be.

Further work

You might like to look at some of the books and films that we've mentioned in this book. They all bring up interesting issues relating to AI.

1984 📖
George Orwell, 1949
2001: A Space Odyssey 🎞
Stanley Kubrick, 1969
AI 🎞
Steven Spielberg, 2001
Bicentennial Man 🎞
Disney, 1999
Frankenstein 📖
Mary Wollstonecroft Shelley, 1818
Inspector Gadget 🎞
Disney, 1999
Pinocchio 📖 🎞
Carlo Lorenzini (pen-name Carlo Collodi), 1883; Disney, 1940
Spy Kids 🎞
Disney, 2001
Star Trek 💬
Gene Roddenberry, 1960s onwards
Star Trek: The Next Generation 💬
Gene Roddenberry, 1987 onwards
Star Wars 🎞
George Lucas, 1977
Star Wars Episode I: Phantom Menace 🎞
George Lucas, 1999
Westworld 🎞
Michael Crichton, 1973
The Wizard of Oz 📖 🎞
Victor Fleming, 1939

An AI manifesto
Science fiction writer Isaac Asimov put together a set of 'laws' that say how an AI or robot should behave:
1 A robot may not injure a human being, or, through inaction, allow a human being to come to harm.
2 A robot must obey the orders given to it by human beings except where such orders would conflict with the First Law.
3 A robot must protect its own existence as long as such protection does not conflict with the First or Second Law.
0 (added later) A robot may not injure humanity, or, through inaction, allow humanity to come to harm.

Make a manifesto

To take your interest in AI further, review the questions you've discussed while reading this book. Make up a manifesto, treaty or series of laws of your own to set out restrictions or guidelines on AI development and use. Circulate your ideas and get comments from other people, then think again about what you've said and decide whether you should make any changes.

Glossary

android A robot that looks and acts like a human.

artificial neural network A computer system that copies the way the human brain works.

autism A medical condition that affects a person's psychological development and prevents them relating to and communicating effectively with others.

automated system A computerised system that works automatically, without a human operator.

bio-bot A robot that is built using soft tissues that look and feel like skin and flesh.

blasphemous Going against a religion or certain religious beliefs.

conscience A moral sense of right and wrong.

consciousness Awareness of one's own existence.

cybernetics The study or development of control systems in machines, computers and living things.

cyborg A person whose body parts or biological functions are enhanced by computer or robot technology.

expert system A computer system with extensive specialist knowledge. An expert system has the ability to reach judgements or conclusions by processing its information using a set of programmed rules.

free will The ability to make independent decisions and act on them.

genetic Relating to genes, which are the means by which we inherit characteristics from our parents and ancestors.

hacker A person who breaks into computer systems, usually to steal or change information.

humanoid Similar to a human in appearance.

IQ (intelligence quotient) test A mental test that includes questions and puzzles designed to judge your ability to recognise, learn and apply patterns, demonstrate logic, think quickly, and see connections between things.

moral Relating to human behaviour, especially the distinction between good and bad and right and wrong.

phonetics The scientific study of speech processes, including pronunciation and speech sounds.

stock market Also called the stock exchange. A global market where shares are bought and sold.

virus (computer) A program designed to destroy or disrupt data and to spread from one computer to another. Viruses can spread very quickly via the Internet.

Index